MW01245485
DREAM
write
CREATE

2015
calendar

JANUARY

S	M	T	W	T	F	S
				1	2	3
4	5	6	7	8	9	10
11	12	13	14	15	16	17
18	19	20	21	22	23	24
25	26	27	28	29	30	31

FEBRUARY

S	M	T	W	T	F	S
1	2	3	4	5	6	7
8	9	10	11	12	13	14
15	16	17	18	19	20	21
22	23	24	25	26	27	28

MARCH

S	M	T	W	T	F	S
1	2	3	4	5	6	7
8	9	10	11	12	13	14
15	16	17	18	19	20	21
22	23	24	25	26	27	28
29	30	31				

APRIL

S	M	T	W	T	F	S
			1	2	3	4
5	6	7	8	9	10	11
12	13	14	15	16	17	18
19	20	21	22	23	24	25
26	27	28	29	30		

MAY

S	M	T	W	T	F	S
					1	2
3	4	5	6	7	8	9
10	11	12	13	14	15	16
17	18	19	20	21	22	23
24	25	26	27	28	29	30
31						

JUNE

S	M	T	W	T	F	S
	1	2	3	4	5	6
7	8	9	10	11	12	13
14	15	16	17	18	19	20
21	22	23	24	25	26	27
28	29	30				

JULY

S	M	T	W	T	F	S
			1	2	3	4
5	6	7	8	9	10	11
12	13	14	15	16	17	18
19	20	21	22	23	24	25
26	27	28	29	30	31	

AUGUST

S	M	T	W	T	F	S
						1
2	3	4	5	6	7	8
9	10	11	12	13	14	15
16	17	18	19	20	21	22
23	24	25	26	27	28	29
30	31					

SEPTEMBER

S	M	T	W	T	F	S
		1	2	3	4	5
6	7	8	9	10	11	12
13	14	15	16	17	18	19
20	21	22	23	24	25	26
27	28	29	30			

OCTOBER

S	M	T	W	T	F	S
				1	2	3
4	5	6	7	8	9	10
11	12	13	14	15	16	17
18	19	20	21	22	23	24
25	26	27	28	29	30	31

NOVEMBER

S	M	T	W	T	F	S
1	2	3	4	5	6	7
8	9	10	11	12	13	14
15	16	17	18	19	20	21
22	23	24	25	26	27	28
29	30					

DECEMBER

S	M	T	W	T	F	S
		1	2	3	4	5
6	7	8	9	10	11	12
13	14	15	16	17	18	19
20	21	22	23	24	25	26
27	28	29	30	31		

2016
calendar

JANUARY

S	M	T	W	T	F	S
					1	2
3	4	5	6	7	8	9
10	11	12	13	14	15	16
17	18	19	20	21	22	23
24	25	26	27	28	29	30
31						

FEBRUARY

S	M	T	W	T	F	S
	1	2	3	4	5	6
7	8	9	10	11	12	13
14	15	16	17	18	19	20
21	22	23	24	25	26	27
28	29					

MARCH

S	M	T	W	T	F	S
		1	2	3	4	5
6	7	8	9	10	11	12
13	14	15	16	17	18	19
20	21	22	23	24	25	26
27	28	29	30	31		

APRIL

S	M	T	W	T	F	S
					1	2
3	4	5	6	7	8	9
10	11	12	13	14	15	16
17	18	19	20	21	22	23
24	25	26	27	28	29	30

MAY

S	M	T	W	T	F	S
1	2	3	4	5	6	7
8	9	10	11	12	13	14
15	16	17	18	19	20	21
22	23	24	25	26	27	28
29	30	31				

JUNE

S	M	T	W	T	F	S
			1	2	3	4
5	6	7	8	9	10	11
12	13	14	15	16	17	18
19	20	21	22	23	24	25
26	27	28	29	30		

JULY

S	M	T	W	T	F	S
					1	2
3	4	5	6	7	8	9
10	11	12	13	14	15	16
17	18	19	20	21	22	23
24	25	26	27	28	29	30
31						

AUGUST

S	M	T	W	T	F	S
	1	2	3	4	5	6
7	8	9	10	11	12	13
14	15	16	17	18	19	20
21	22	23	24	25	26	27
28	29	30	31			

SEPTEMBER

S	M	T	W	T	F	S
				1	2	3
4	5	6	7	8	9	10
11	12	13	14	15	16	17
18	19	20	21	22	23	24
25	26	27	28	29	30	

OCTOBER

S	M	T	W	T	F	S
						1
2	3	4	5	6	7	8
9	10	11	12	13	14	15
16	17	18	19	20	21	22
23	24	25	26	27	28	29
30	31					

NOVEMBER

S	M	T	W	T	F	S
		1	2	3	4	5
6	7	8	9	10	11	12
13	14	15	16	17	18	19
20	21	22	23	24	25	26
27	28	29	30			

DECEMBER

S	M	T	W	T	F	S
				1	2	3
4	5	6	7	8	9	10
11	12	13	14	15	16	17
18	19	20	21	22	23	24
25	26	27	28	29	30	31

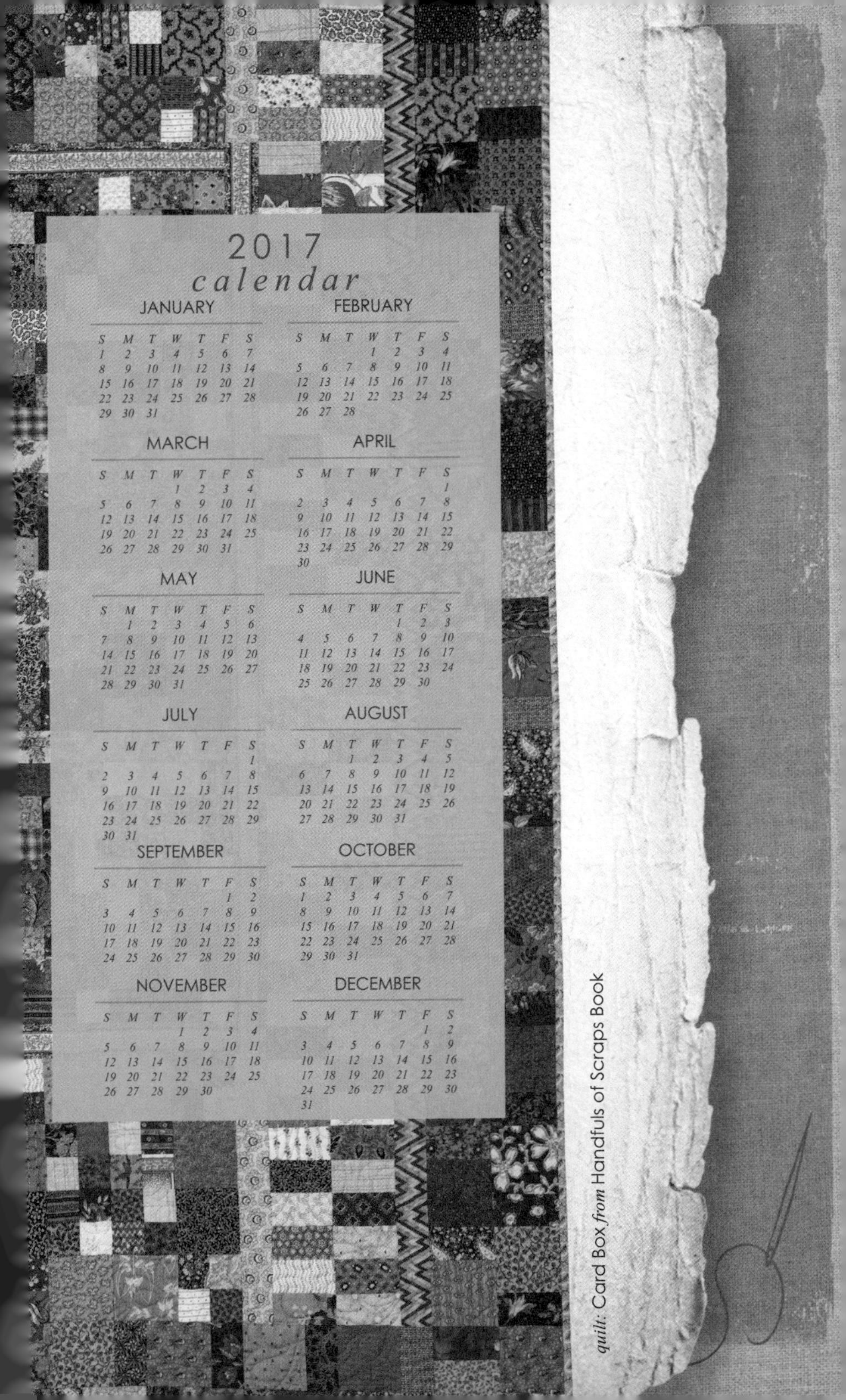

quilt: Card Box *from* Handfuls of Scraps Book

monday

tuesday

wednesday

quilt: Super-Simple Four Patch *from* Handfuls of Scraps Book

thursday

friday

saturday

sunday

monday

tuesday

wednesday

THINK LESS

quilt more

thursday

friday

saturday

sunday

quilt: Let it Shine *from* Handfuls of Scraps Book

journal

monday

tuesday

wednesday

quilt: Flower Garden *from* Handfuls of Scraps Book

thursday

friday

saturday

sunday

monday

tuesday

wednesday

ALL FUN
AND GAMES
*until your
thread
runs out*

thursday

friday

saturday

sunday

quilt: Slow and Steady *from* Handfuls of Scraps Book

SEW AND *dream*

monday

tuesday

wednesday

quilt: Sunrise Scraps *from* Handfuls of Scraps Book

thursday

friday

saturday

sunday

monday

tuesday

wednesday

ENJOY
life

quilt: Bubblegum *from* Reasons for Quilts Book

thursday

friday

saturday

sunday

monday

tuesday

wednesday

LIVE

piecefully

thursday

friday

saturday

sunday

quilt: Bow Tie *from* Handfuls of Sraps Book

monday

tuesday

wednesday

quilt: Scraps on Parade *from* Handfuls of Scraps Book

sew happy

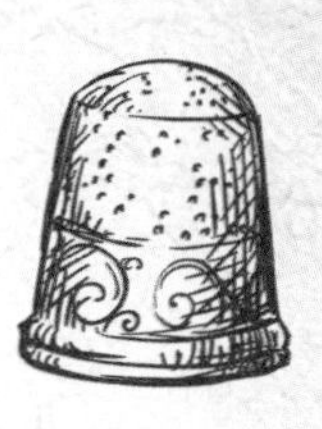

thursday

friday

saturday

sunday

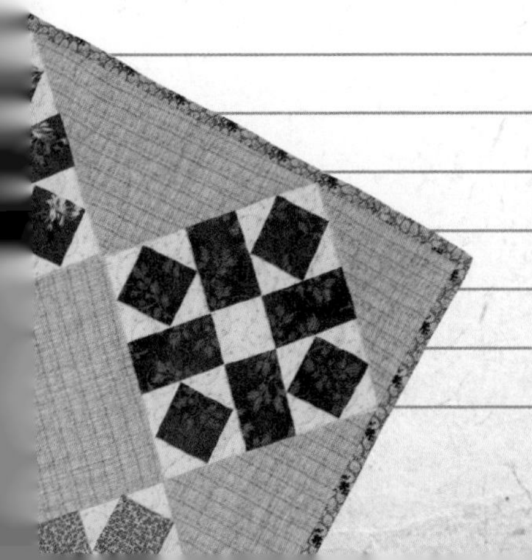

monday

tuesday

wednesday

thursday

MAY YOUR BOBBIN *always be full*

quilt: Sweet Sixteen *from* Laundry Basket Quilts Pattern

friday

saturday

sunday

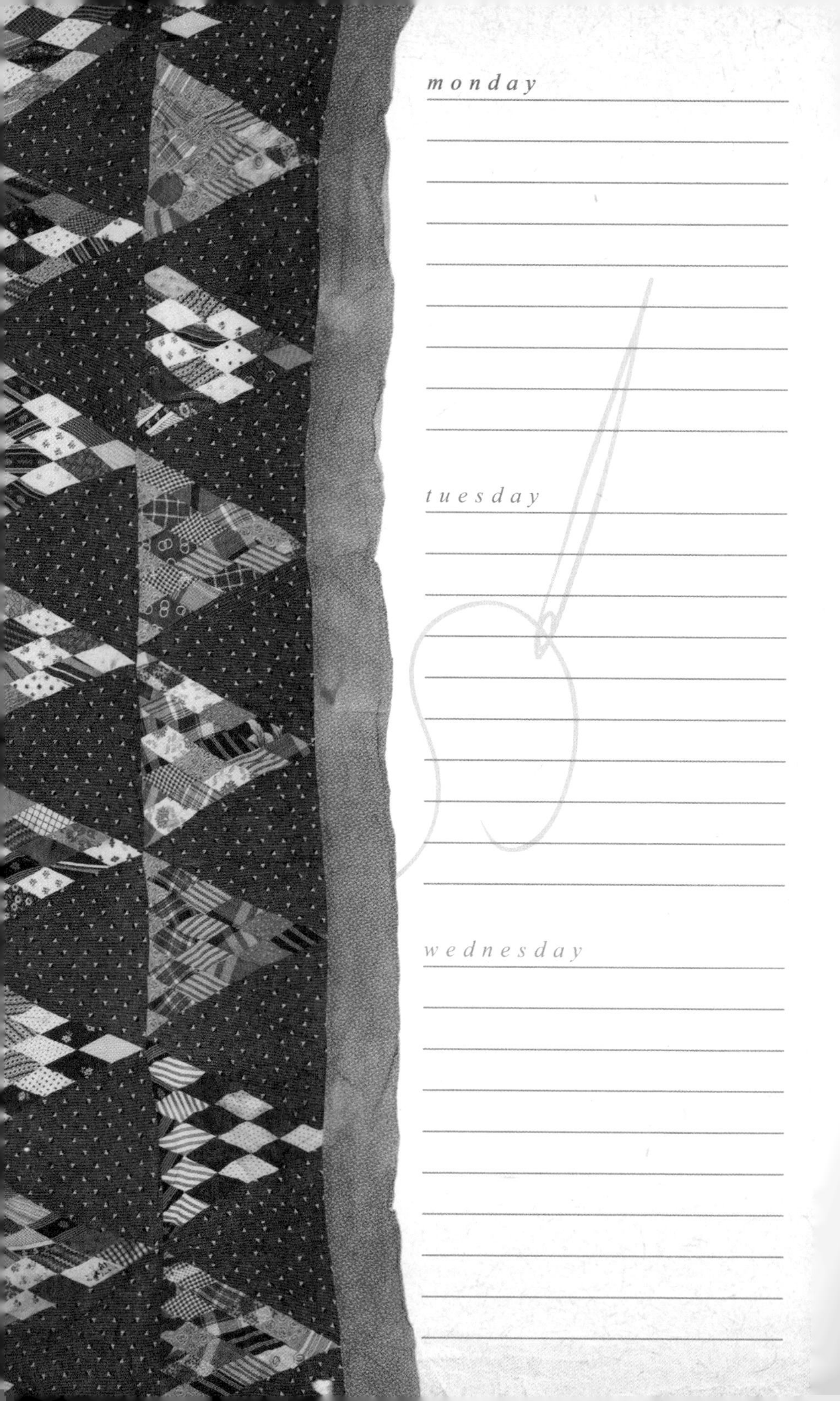

monday

tuesday

wednesday

thursday

friday

saturday

sunday

quilt: Diamond at Night *from* Handfuls of Scraps Book

monday

tuesday

wednesday

thursday

friday

saturday

sunday

quilt: Eldon *from* Laundry Basket Quilts Pattern

monday

tuesday

wednesday

dream big!

thursday

friday

saturday

sunday

quilt: Love at First Sight *from* Handfuls of Scraps Book

monday

tuesday

wednesday

thursday

friday

saturday

sunday

write

quilt: Midnight Bloom *from* Laundry Basket Quilts Pattern

monday

tuesday

wednesday

MEASURE TWICE
cut once

thursday

friday

saturday

sunday

quilt: Sunset *from* Laundry Basket Quilts Pattern

HAPPY quilting
monday
tuesday
wednesday

thursday

friday

saturday

sunday

quilt: Appliqué Affair *from* Laundry Basket Quilts Pattern

monday

tuesday

wednesday

thursday

friday

saturday

sunday

quilt: Stars Upon Stars *from* Handfuls of Scraps Book

BIG PROJECTS *start with little pieces*

monday

tuesday

wednesday

quilt: Card Box *from* Handfuls of Scraps Book

thursday

friday

saturday

sunday

monday

tuesday

wednesday

quilt: Boisterous Bear *from* Laundry Basket Quilts Pattern

thursday

friday

saturday

sunday

quilt

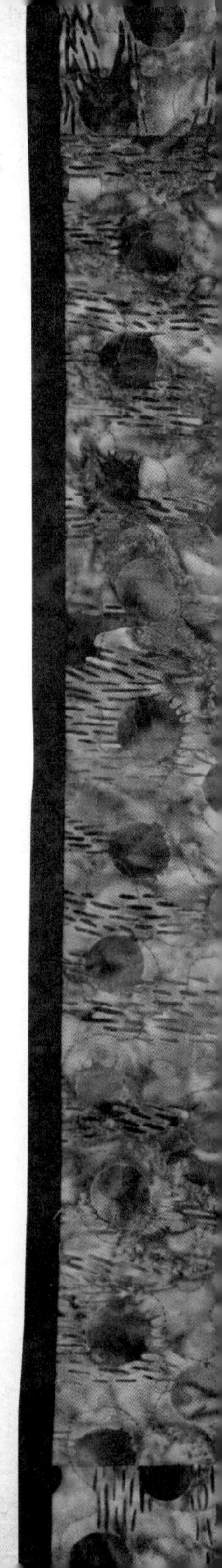

monday
tuesday
wednesday
thursday

friday

saturday

sunday

SCRAPS

don't have to match

quilt: Pink Broken Dish *from* Handfuls of Scraps Book

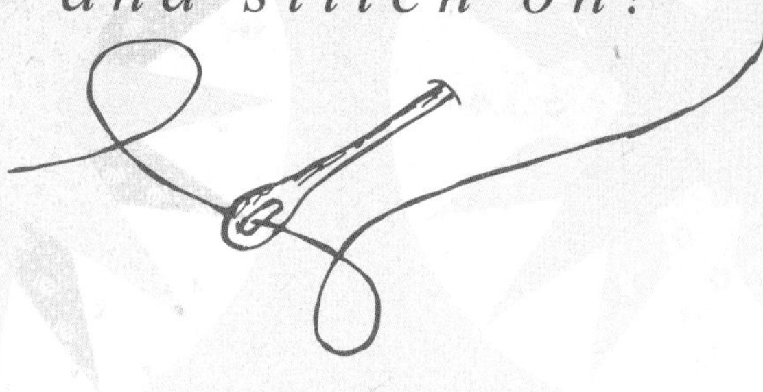

monday

tuesday

wednesday

quilt: Compass Quilt ***from*** Reasons for Quilts Book

thursday

friday

saturday

sunday

monday

tuesday

wednesday

thursday

quilt: Basket of Scraps *from* Handfuls of Scraps Book

friday

saturday

sunday

when life gives you scraps MAKE A QUILT

quilt: Nine Patch with Flower Basket Border *from* Handfuls of Scraps Book

monday

tuesday

wednesday

thursday

friday

saturday

sunday

monday

tuesday

wednesday

thursday

friday

saturday

sunday

quilt: Sunflower *from* Laundry Basket Quilts Pattern

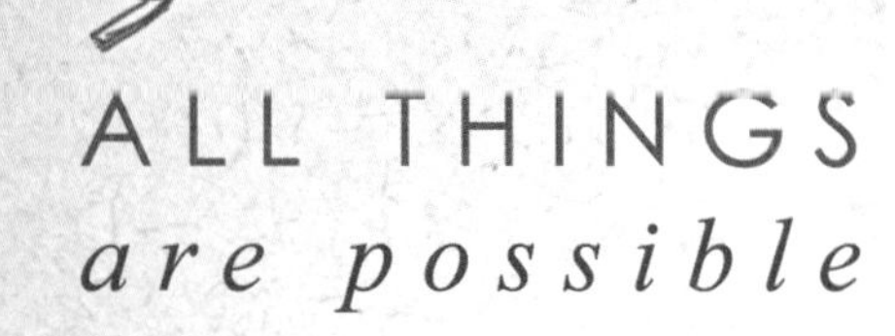

ALL THINGS *are possible*

monday

tuesday

wednesday

quilt: Broken Dish *from* Handfuls of Scraps Book

thursday

friday

saturday

sunday

monday

tuesday

wednesday

thursday

friday

saturday

sunday

quilt: Rolling Stone *from* Handfuls of Scraps Book

monday

tuesday

wednesday

hope

thursday

friday

saturday

sunday

quilt: Gather 'Round *from* Handfuls of Scraps Book

SEWING
mends the soul
monday
tuesday
wednesday

thursday

friday

saturday

sunday

quilt: Monkey Business *from* Handfuls of Scraps Book

monday

tuesday

wednesday

DO MORE
of what makes you happy

thursday

friday

saturday

sunday

quilt: Scraps on Parade *from* Handfuls of Scraps Book

HAPPY *stitches*

monday

tuesday

wednesday

create

quilt: Recycled Beauty *from* Reasons for Quilts Book

thursday

friday

saturday

sunday

monday

tuesday

wednesday

thursday

quilt: Valentine's Goodies *from* Reasons for Quilts Book

friday

saturday

sunday

STITCH
your stress away

monday

tuesday

wednesday

STITCH

with love

thursday

friday

saturday

sunday

quilt: Wild Goose Chase *from* Handfuls of Scraps Book

monday

tuesday

wednesday

love in stitches

thursday

friday

saturday

sunday

quilt: Nine Patch Variation *from* Handfuls of Scraps Book

YOUR STITCHES DON'T
HAVE TO BE PERFECT
to enjoy them

monday

tuesday

wednesday

thursday

friday

saturday

sunday

quilt: Flower Garden *from* Handfuls of Scraps Book

monday

tuesday

wednesday

thursday

friday

saturday

sunday

quilt: Rocking Chair Quilt *from* Reasons for Quilts Book

monday

tuesday

wednesday

thursday

friday

saturday

sunday

quilt: Double Dare *from* Reasons for Quilts Book

monday

tuesday

wednesday

you are sew special

thursday

friday

saturday

sunday

quilt: Looking Glass *from* Handfuls of Scraps Book

monday
tuesday
wednesday
thursday

friday

saturday

sunday

CLOSE TO
my heart

quilt: Crazy in Love Medallion *from* Handfuls of Scraps Book

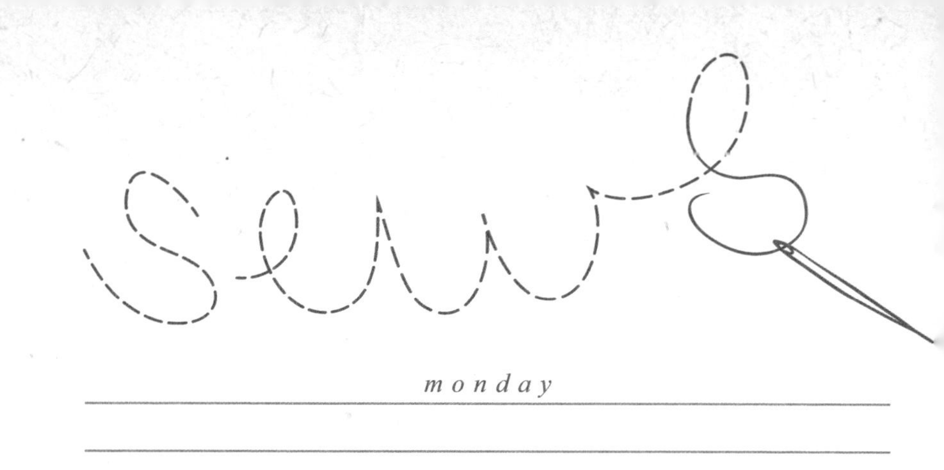

monday

tuesday

wednesday

thursday

friday

saturday

sunday

quilt: Barn Raising Log Cabin *from* Handfuls of Scraps Book

monday

tuesday

wednesday

handmade

quilt: The Hand-off *from* Reasons for Quilts Book

monday

tuesday

wednesday

thursday

friday

saturday

sunday

quilt: Poppies *from* Laundry Basket Quilts Pattern

LIFE IS HARD
but beautiful

monday

tuesday

wednesday

quilt: Four Patch *from* Handfuls of Scraps Book

thursday

friday

saturday

sunday

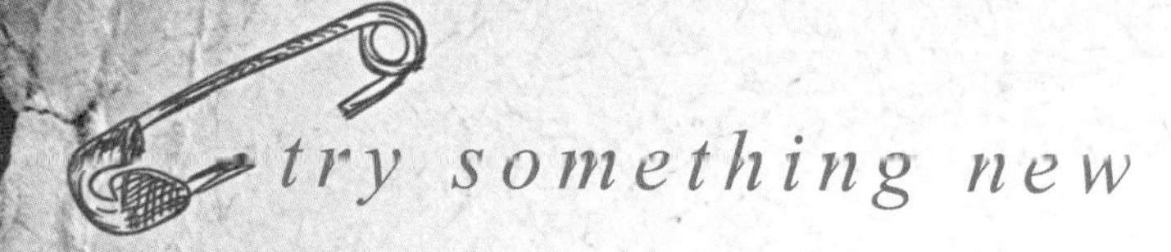

try something new

monday

tuesday

wednesday

quilt: Bear Claw *from* Handfuls of Scraps Book

thursday

friday

saturday

sunday

quilt

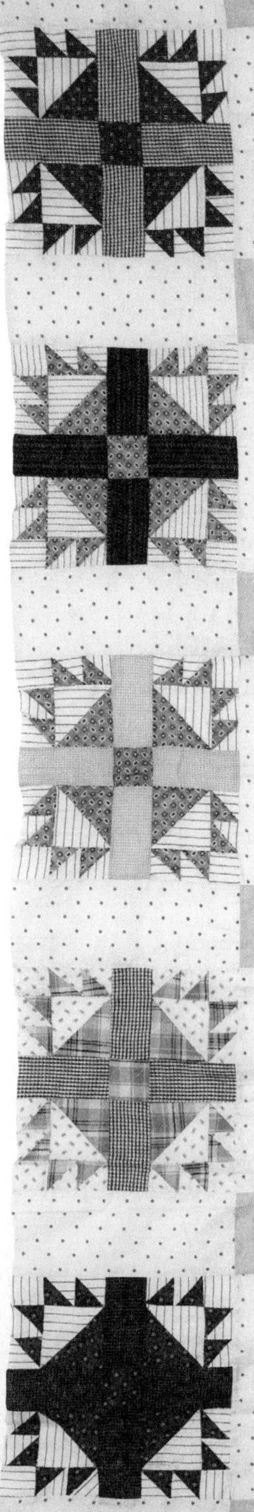

monday

tuesday

wednesday

thursday

friday

saturday

sunday

HAPPINESS
is fabric

quilt: Monkey Business *from* Handfuls of Scraps Book

COMFORT *with love*

monday

tuesday

wednesday

quilt: Sunflower ***from*** Handfuls of Scraps Book

thursday

friday

saturday

sunday

monday

tuesday

wednesday

thursday

quilt: Pineapple Quilt *from* Handfuls of Scraps Book

friday

saturday

sunday

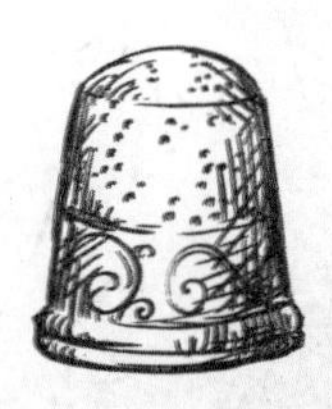

be someone's
REASON TO
SMILE

quilt: Slow and Steady *from* Handfuls of Scraps Book

monday

tuesday

wednesday

thursday

friday

saturday

sunday

monday

tuesday

wednesday

thursday

friday

saturday

sunday

quilt: Holding On *from* Laundry Basket Quilts Pattern

with confidence

monday

tuesday

wednesday

quilt: Christmas Joy *from* Reasons for Quilts Book

thursday

friday

saturday

sunday

monday

tuesday

wednesday

thursday

quilt: Four Patch Trip Around the World *from* Handfuls of Scraps Book

THREAD + FABRIC = *heaven*

monday

tuesday

wednesday

thursday

quilt: Texas Star *from* Handfuls of Scraps Book

friday

saturday

sunday

monday

tuesday

wednesday

be yourself

thursday

friday

saturday

sunday

quilt: Mountain Top *from* Laundry Basket Quilts Pattern

loving stitches

Blanket Stitch

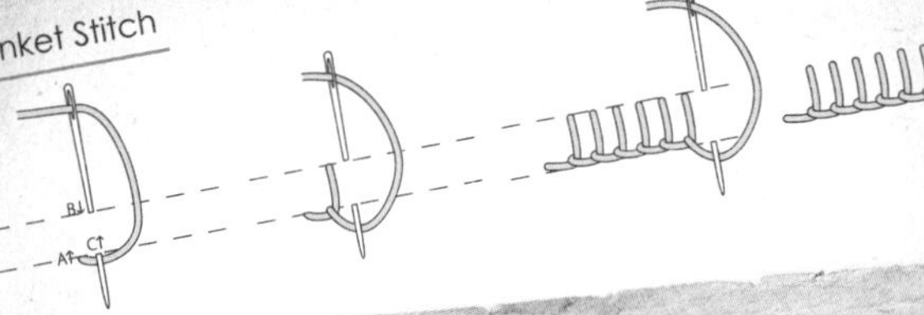

Back Stitch

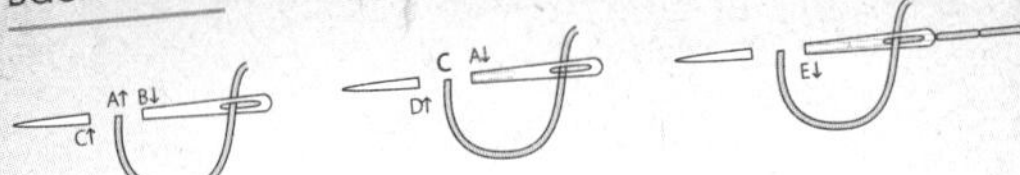

Lazy Daisy

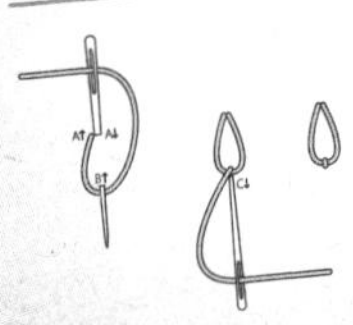

Chain Stitch

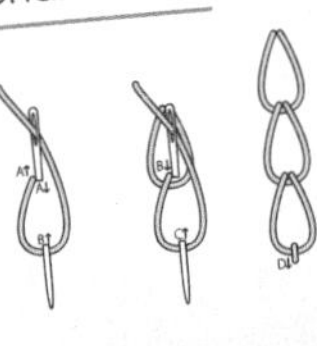

Stem Stitch

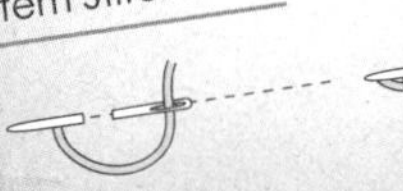

French Stitch

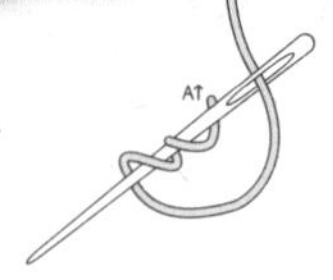

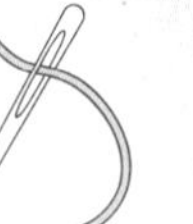

Sheaf Stitch

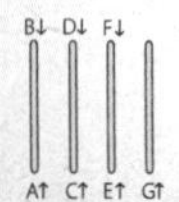

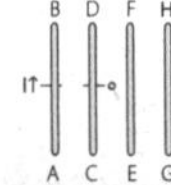

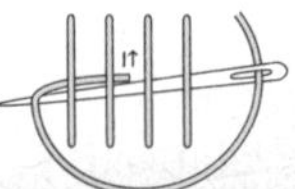

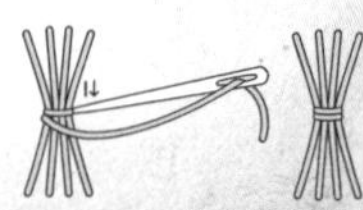

quilt: Piano Key Medallion *from* Handfuls of Scraps Book

GRID *paper*

GRID *paper*

quilt: Squared *from* Handfuls of Scraps Book

GRID *paper*

GRID *paper*

quilt: Love at First Sight *from* Handfuls of Scraps Book

GRID *paper*

GRID *paper*

quilt: Appliqué Affair *from* Laundry Basket Quilts Pattern

GRID *paper*

GRID *paper*

quilt: Scraps on Parade *from* Handfuls of Scraps Book

GRID *paper*

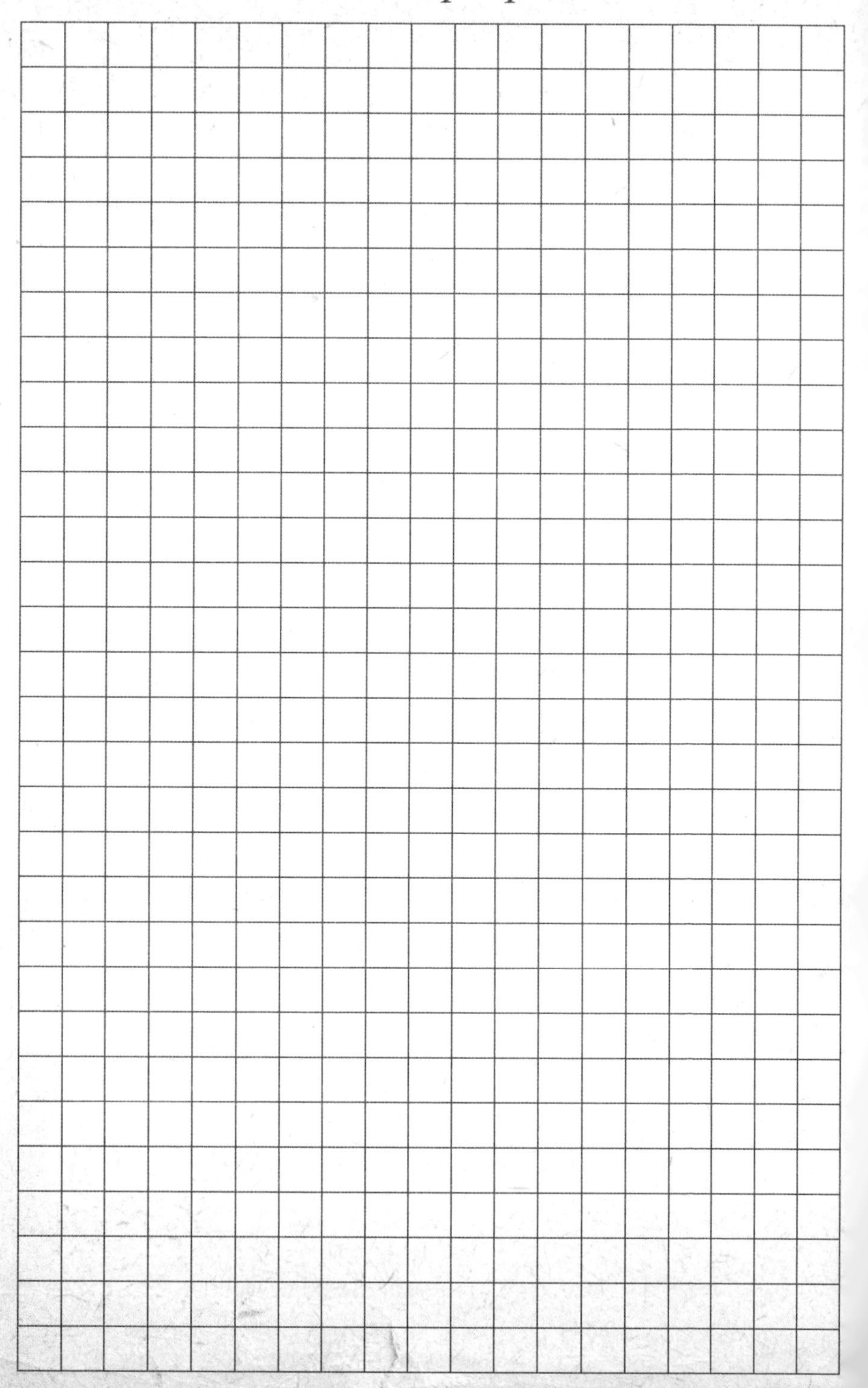

GRID *paper*

From a Fat Quarter (18" x 22")
You can cut:

99 - 2" squares
56 - 2.5" squares
42 - 3" squares
30 - 3.5" squares
20 - 4" squares
16 - 4.5" squares
12 - 5" squares
12 - 5.5" squares
9 - 6" squares
6 - 6.5" squares

Yard	Inches
1/8	4 1/2"
1/4	9"
1/3	12"
3/8	13 1/2"
1/2	18"
5/8	22 1/2"
2/3	24"
3/4	27"
7/8	31 1/2"
1	36"

Bed, Quilting & Batting sizes

bed size	mattress size	quilt size	batting size
crib	27" x 52"	36" x 54"	45" x 60"
twin	39" x 75"	54" x 90"	81" x 96"
full	54" x 75"	72" x 90"	90" x 108"
queen	60" x 80"	90" x 108"	120" x 120"
king	76" x 80"	108" x 108"	120" x 120"

quilt: Bow Tie *from* Handfuls of Scraps Book

notes

quilt: Bubblegum *from* Reasons for Quilts Book

notes

made with love

notes

quilt: Love at First Sight *from* Handfuls of Scraps Book

notes

be thankful

notes

quilt: Compass Quilt *from* Reasons for Quilts Book

notes
make a quilt

notes

quilt: Prairie Stitches *from* Handfuls of Scraps Book

NEVER STOP
dreaming

MEET *the* DESIGNER
Edyta Sitar

Edyta's lifelong relationship with fabric began in Poland at a very young age, when she cut her mother's drapes to design her first project. Fortunately, for all of us, Edyta's mother recognized her passion for fabric that would later unfold into a consummate gift.

One of Edyta's dearest blessings is her marriage to her husband, Michael—and connection to the Sitar family quilting tradition. Both her mother-in-law, Carol, and grandmother-in-law, Anna, sat with Edyta over the quilt frame to teach her the ins and outs of quilting—and the ups and downs of life. With the help of two generations of Sitar women, Edyta found her confidence in this cottage craft, not only as a boundless creative outlet, but also as a means to filter her passion.

In observing the beauty of things around her, experiencing the thrills and challenges of being a woman, and reflecting profoundly on the human condition, Edyta expresses her existence through quilts.

Edyta's intuitive feel for fabric, keen eye for color, and family teachings all contribute to her amazing quilts and natural evolution to pattern and fabric designing. Now working as owner and co-founder of Laundry Basket Quilts (www.laundrybasketquilts.com), Edyta has created close to 150 quilt patterns, traditional and batik fabrics with Moda, and threads, stencils, and templates for quilting. Her most recent innovations include ready-to-appliqué, fusible, laser-cut fabric shapes, ideal for quilting and handwork.

Edyta has documented her quilting stories in her 2011 book *Reasons for Quilts*. She has been published in national magazines and books, and has been featured on *The Quilt Show*. She spreads her quilter's spirit through ongoing workshops, presentations, and classes, including the popular *Craftsy* online creative forum (craftsy.com). Her newest book *Handfuls of Scraps* expresses artistry in the smallest bits of fabric.

She enjoys gardening and small-town living in Michigan with her husband Michael and three children. "My children and my husband are my greatest motivation," she says. "This is a Cinderella dream for me. Being able to do what I love and share this love with others is the greatest feeling and reward I could imagine!"

Other books by Edyta Sitar:

Hop To It! (Landauer, 2009)
Friendship Triangles (Landauer, 2009)
Friendship Strips and Scraps (Landauer, 2010)
Reasons for Quilts (Laundry Basket Quilts, 2011)
Scrappy Fireworks (Landauer, 2012)
Seasonal Silhouettes (Landauer, 2013)
Rainbow Nest (Landauer, 2014)
Handfuls of Scraps (Laundry Basket Quilts, 2014)

For patterns and more information visit Laundry Basket Quilts' website at www.laundrybasketquilts.com

This book was designed, produced, and published by Sitar Family Traditions LLC, DBA: Laundry Basket Quilts, 16860 L Drive North, Marshall, MI 49068
www.laundrybasketquilts.com

Publisher: Sitar Family Traditions LLC, Laundry Basket Quilts
Quilt Design: Edyta Sitar
Sales & Operations: Michael Sitar
Art Director: Kayleen Hardy, Hardy Design Studio
Photography: Michael Sitar, Laundry Basket Quilts
Technical Illustrations: Lisa Christensen

ISBN 13: 978-0-9836688-2-4

This book is printed on acid-free paper.
Printed in the United States of America.
10 9 8 7 6 5 4 3 2 1

quilt: Let it Shine *from* Handfuls of Scraps Book